San Gabriel & Pomona Valley
YOUTH FOR CHRIST, INC.
601 E. Edna Place
Covina, Calif.

The Life of Christ Jesus

in

Bible Language

FROM

THE KING JAMES VERSION OF THE BIBLE

COMPILED BY

GENEVIEVE P. OLSON

FOURTH EDITION, REVISED

PUBLISHED BY

GENEVIEVE P. OLSON

BONITA, CALIFORNIA, U. S. A.

PRINTED IN U.S.A.
ARTS AND CRAFTS PRESS
SAN DIEGO, CALIFORNIA

CONTENTS

PREFACE

IN rearing four children the author often read to them from the King James Version of the Bible, selecting passages to tell the complete stories of various Bible characters. Incidents pertaining to the life of Christ Jesus were also read, together with his teachings and healings.

Not only did they gain an understanding of the spiritual value of the Bible, but the children acquired a fine sense of rhythm, poesy and diction from the beautiful language of the King James Version, the simplicity of which even a child can understand.

For many years the author aspired to write a child's life of Christ Jesus. One day it came to her thought, "What could be more beautiful and inspiring than the story written in Bible language!" And this little volume is humbly offered as fruitage.

The subject has been approached reverently, and the author believes that the book will hold the interest of adults as well as young people, and that it will prove helpful to Bible students of any age.

Each chapter portrays some phase of the Master's life, and the events recorded in each chapter are arranged chronologically (according to the "Oxford Encyclopedic Concordance" and "Hurlburt's Bible Encyclopaedia") with the exception of the chapter, "Some of Jesus' Teachings and Parables," which has been compiled according to subject matter rather than in accordance with the sequence in which Jesus' words were spoken. It is believed that this arrangement gives continuity of thought to this chapter.

PREFACE

Obviously, many incidents in the Master's life, and many of the teachings and healings have had to be omitted in order to keep the story from being tedious to the young reader; nevertheless, the author believes that a vivid and authentic portrayal of the life and works of Christ Jesus has been accomplished.

Although the book is divided into paragraphs instead of verses, the Bible language and punctuation have been meticulously conformed to. Except for a few parenthesized words which have necessarily been inserted to bring out the meaning of the context, every word is from the King James Version of the Bible. References of all selections are given in the margins.

The italicized words in this volume are the same as those in the Authorized Version. It is said by Bible authorities, that these italicized words indicate insertions which the translators believed would clarify the meaning of the original text.

Since the publication of the first edition, slight revisions and pertinent additions have been made which add significant details to related events, especially in the final chapters.

It is devoutely hoped that this little volume will bring to those who read it a deeper appreciation of the King James Version of the Bible, and a better understanding of Christ Jesus.

GENEVIEVE P. OLSON

For other foundation
can no man lay
than is laid,
which is Jesus Christ.

I CORINTHIANS 3: 11

The Annunciation

PROPHESY: Isaiah 7:14 Therefore the Lord himself shall give you a sign; Behold, a virgin shall conceive, and bear a son, and shall call his name Immanuel.

❧〰〰〰〰❧

AND in the sixth month the angel Gabriel was sent from God unto a city of Galilee, named Nazareth, to a virgin espoused to a man whose name was Joseph, of the house of David; and the virgin's name *was* Mary. Luke 1: 26-35, 38-42, 46-48

And the angel came in unto her, and said, Hail, *thou that art* highly favoured, the Lord *is* with thee: blessed *art* thou among women.

And when she saw *him,* she was troubled at his saying, and cast in her mind what manner of salutation this should be.

And the angel said unto her, Fear not, Mary: for thou hast found favour with God. And, behold, thou shalt conceive in thy womb, and bring forth a son, and shalt call his name JESUS. He shall be great, and shall be called the Son of the Highest: and the Lord God shall give unto him the throne of his father David: and he shall reign over the house of Jacob for ever; and of his kingdom there shall be no end.

Then said Mary unto the angel, How shall this be, seeing I know not a man?

And the angel answered and said unto her, The Holy Ghost shall come upon thee, and the power of

1

the Highest shall overshadow thee: therefore also that holy thing which shall be born of thee shall be called the Son of God.

And Mary said, Behold the handmaid of the Lord; be it unto me according to thy word.

And the angel departed from her.

And Mary arose in those days, and went into the hill country with haste, into a city of Juda; and entered into the house of Zacharias, and saluted Elizabeth. And it came to pass, that, when Elizabeth heard the salutation of Mary, . . . Elizabeth was filled with the Holy Ghost: and she spake out with a loud voice, and said, Blessed *art* thou among women, and blessed *is* the fruit of thy womb.

And Mary said, My soul doth magnify the Lord, and my spirit hath rejoiced in God my Saviour. For he hath regarded the low estate of his handmaiden: for, behold, from henceforth all generations shall call me blessed.

The Birth of Jesus

PROPHESY: Isaiah 9:6 For unto us a child is born, unto us a son is given: and the government shall be upon his shoulder: and his name shall be called Wonderful, Counsellor, The mighty God, The everlasting Father, The Prince of Peace.

AND the Word was made flesh, and dwelt among us, (and we beheld his glory, the glory as of the only begotten of the Father,) full of grace and truth. *John 1: 14*

But when the fulness of the time was come, God sent forth his Son, made of a woman, made under the law, to redeem them that were under the law, that we might receive the adoption of sons. *Galatians 4: 4, 5*

Now the birth of Jesus Christ was on this wise: When as his mother Mary was espoused to Joseph, before they came together, she was found with child of the Holy Ghost. *Matthew 1: 18-22*

Then Joseph her husband, being a just *man,* and not willing to make her a publick example, was minded to put her away privily. But while he thought on these things, behold, the angel of the Lord appeared unto him in a dream, saying, Joseph, thou son of David, fear not to take unto thee Mary thy wife: for that which is conceived in her is of the Holy Ghost. And she shall bring forth a son, and thou shalt call his name JESUS: for he shall save his people from their sins.

Now all this was done, that it might be fulfilled which was spoken of the Lord by the prophet . . .

And it came to pass in those days, that there went out *Luke 2: 1*

3

Luke 2:
4-20, 22,
25-32

a decree from Cæsar Augustus, that all the world should be taxed. And Joseph also went up from Galilee, out of the city of Nazareth, into Judæa, unto the city of David, which is called Bethlehem; (because he was of the house and lineage of David:) to be taxed with Mary his espoused wife, being great with child.

And so it was, that, while they were there, the days were accomplished that she should be delivered. And she brought forth her firstborn son, and wrapped him in swaddling clothes, and laid him in a manger; because there was no room for them in the inn.

And there were in the same country shepherds abiding in the field, keeping watch over their flock by night. And, lo, the angel of the Lord came upon them, and the glory of the Lord shone round about them: and they were sore afraid.

And the angel said unto them, Fear not: for, behold, I bring you good tidings of great joy, which shall be to all people. For unto you is born this day in the city of David a Saviour, which is Christ the Lord. And this *shall be* a sign unto you; Ye shall find the babe wrapped in swaddling clothes, lying in a manger.

And suddenly there was with the angel a multitude of the heavenly host praising God, and saying, Glory to God in the highest, and on earth peace, good will toward men.

And ... the shepherds said one to another, Let us now go even unto Bethlehem, and see this thing which is come to pass, which the Lord hath made known unto us.

And they came with haste, and found Mary, and Joseph, and the babe lying in a manger. And when they had seen *it,* they made known abroad the saying which was told them concerning this child. And all they that

4

THE BIRTH OF JESUS

heard *it* wondered at those things which were told them by the shepherds. But Mary kept all these things, and pondered *them* in her heart.

And the shepherds returned, glorifying and praising God for all the things that they had heard and seen, as it was told unto them.

And when the days of (Mary's) purification according to the law of Moses were accomplished, they brought (the babe) to Jerusalem, to present *him* to the Lord; and, behold, there was a man in Jerusalem, whose name *was* Simeon; and the same man *was* just and devout, waiting for the consolation of Israel: and the Holy Ghost was upon him. And it was revealed unto him by the Holy Ghost, that he should not see death, before he had seen the Lord's Christ.

And he came by the Spirit into the temple: and when the parents brought in the child Jesus, to do for him after the custom of the law, then (Simeon) took . . . him up in his arms, and blessed God, and said, Lord, now lettest thou thy servant depart in peace, according to thy word: for mine eyes have seen thy salvation, which thou hast prepared before the face of all people; a light to lighten the Gentiles, and the glory of thy people Israel.

Now when Jesus was born in Bethlehem of Judæa in the days of Herod the king, behold, there came wise men from the east to Jerusalem, saying, Where is he that is born King of the Jews? for we have seen his star in the east, and are come to worship him.

When Herod the king had heard *these things,* he was troubled, and all Jerusalem with him. And when he had gathered all the chief priests and scribes of the people together, he demanded of them where Christ should be born.

Matthew 2: 1-15

5

And they said unto him, In Bethlehem of Judæa: for thus it is written by the prophet, And thou Bethlehem, *in* the land of Juda, art not the least among the princes of Juda: for out of thee shall come a Governor, that shall rule my people Israel.

Then Herod, when he had privily called the wise men, enquired of them diligently what time the star appeared. And he sent them to Bethlehem, and said, Go and search diligently for the young child; and when ye have found *him,* bring me word again, that I may come and worship him also.

When they had heard the king, they departed; and, lo, the star, which they saw in the east, went before them, till it came and stood over where the young child was. When they saw the star, they rejoiced with exceeding great joy. And when they were come into the house, they saw the young child with Mary his mother, and fell down, and worshipped him: and when they had opened their treasures, they presented unto him gifts; gold, and frankincense, and myrrh.

And being warned of God in a dream that they should not return to Herod, they departed into their own country another way. And when they were departed, behold, the angel of the Lord appeareth to Joseph in a dream, saying, Arise, and take the young child and his mother, and flee into Egypt, and be thou there until I bring thee word: for Herod will seek the young child to destroy him.

When he arose, he took the young child and his mother by night, and departed into Egypt: and was there until the death of Herod: that it might be fulfilled which was spoken of the Lord by the prophet, saying, Out of Egypt have I called my son.

The Childhood of Jesus

PROPHESY: Isaiah 11:1, 2 And there shall come forth a rod out of the stem of Jesse, and a Branch shall grow out of his roots: and the spirit of the Lord shall rest upon him, the spirit of wisdom and understanding, the spirit of counsel and might, the spirit of knowledge and of the fear of the Lord;

Isaiah 53:2 For he shall grow up before him as a tender plant, and as a root out of a dry ground: he hath no form nor comeliness; and when we shall see him, *there is* no beauty that we should desire him.

Psalms 45:2 Thou art fairer than the children of men: grace is poured into thy lips: therefore God hath blessed thee for ever.

BUT when Herod was dead, behold, an angel of the Lord appeareth in a dream to Joseph in Egypt, saying, Arise, and take the young child and his mother, and go into the land of Israel: for they are dead which sought the young child's life.   Matthew 2: 19-21, 23

And he arose, and took the young child and his mother, and came into the land of Israel. And he came and dwelt in a city called Nazareth: that it might be fulfilled which was spoken by the prophets, He shall be called a Nazarene.

And the child grew, and waxed strong in spirit, filled with wisdom: and the grace of God was upon him.   Luke 2: 40-49, 51, 52

7

Now his parents went to Jerusalem every year at the feast of the passover. And when he was twelve years old, they went up to Jerusalem after the custom of the feast. And when they had fulfilled the days, as they returned, the child Jesus tarried behind in Jerusalem; and Joseph and his mother knew not *of it*. But they, supposing him to have been in the company, went a day's journey; and they sought him among *their* kinsfolk and acquaintance. And when they found him not, they turned back again to Jerusalem, seeking him.

And it came to pass, that after three days they found him in the temple, sitting in the midst of the doctors, both hearing them, and asking them questions. And all that heard him were astonished at his understanding and answers.

And when they saw him, they were amazed: and his mother said unto him, Son, why hast thou thus dealt with us? behold, thy father and I have sought thee sorrowing.

And he said unto them, How is it that ye sought me? wist ye not that I must be about my Father's business?

And he went down with them, and came to Nazareth, and was subject unto them: but his mother kept all these sayings in her heart. And Jesus increased in wisdom and stature, and in favour with God and man.

Jesus' Preparation

PROPHESY: Malachi 3:1 Behold, I will send my messenger, and he shall prepare the way before me: . . . Isaiah 40:3 The voice of him that crieth in the wilderness, Prepare ye the way of the Lord, . . . Isaiah 52:13 Behold, my servant shall deal prudently, he shall be exalted and extolled, and be very high.

IN those days came John the Baptist, preaching in the wilderness of Judæa, and saying, Repent ye: for the kingdom of heaven is at hand.

Matthew 3: 1, 2

And as the people were in expectation, and all men mused in their hearts of John, whether he were the Christ, or not; John answered, saying unto *them* all, I indeed baptize you with water; but one mightier than I cometh, the latchet of whose shoes I am not worthy to unloose: he shall baptize you with the Holy Ghost and with fire.

Luke 3: 15, 16

The next day John seeth Jesus coming unto him, and saith, Behold the Lamb of God, which taketh away the sin of the world.

John 1: 29

Then cometh Jesus from Galilee to Jordan unto John, to be baptized of him. But John forbad him, saying, I have need to be baptized of thee, and comest thou to me?

Matthew 3: 13-17

And Jesus answering said unto him, Suffer *it to be so* now: for thus it becometh us to fulfil all righteousness.

Then he suffered him.

And Jesus, when he was baptized, went up straightway out of the water: and, lo, the heavens were opened unto him, and he saw the Spirit of God descending like a dove, and lighting upon him: and lo a voice from heaven, saying, This is my beloved Son, in whom I am well pleased.

Luke 4: 1-4

And Jesus being full of the Holy Ghost returned from Jordan, and was led by the Spirit into the wilderness, being forty days tempted of the devil. And in those days he did eat nothing: and when they were ended, he afterward hungered.

And the devil said unto him, If thou be the Son of God, command this stone that it be made bread.

And Jesus answered him, saying, It is written, That man shall not live by bread alone, but by every word of God.

Matthew 4: 5-11

Then the devil taketh him up into the holy city, and setteth him on a pinnacle of the temple, and saith unto him, If thou be the Son of God, cast thyself down: for it is written, He shall give his angels charge concerning thee: and in *their* hands they shall bear thee up, lest at any time thou dash thy foot against a stone.

Jesus said unto him, It is written again, Thou shalt not tempt the Lord thy God.

Again, the devil taketh him up into an exceeding high mountain, and sheweth him all the kingdoms of the world, and the glory of them; and saith unto him, All these things will I give thee, if thou wilt fall down and worship me.

Then saith Jesus unto him, Get thee hence, Satan: for it is written, Thou shalt worship the Lord thy God, and him only shalt thou serve.

Then the devil leaveth him, and, behold, angels came and ministered unto him.

❧❧❧

Thou has loved righteousness, and hated iniquity; therefore God, *even* thy God, hath annointed thee with the oil of gladness above thy fellows. Hebrews 1: 9

For we have not an high priest which cannot be touched with the feeling of our infirmities; but was in all points tempted like as *we are, yet* without sin. Hebrews 4: 15

Let no man say when he is tempted, I am tempted of God: for God cannot be tempted with evil, neither tempteth he any man. James 1: 13

The Healing Ministry of Jesus

PROPHESY: Isaiah 52:9, 10 Break forth into joy, sing together, ye waste places of Jerusalem: for the Lord hath comforted his people, he hath redeemed Jerusalem. The Lord hath made bare is holy arm in the eyes of all the nations; and all the ends of the earth shall see the salvation of our God.

Isaiah 35:5, 6 Then the eyes of the blind shall be opened, and the ears of the deaf shall be unstopped. Then shall the lame *man* leap as an hart, and the tongue of the dumb sing: for in the wilderness shall waters break out, and streams in the desert.

John 2: 11-13, 23

THIS beginning of miracles did Jesus in Cana of Galilee, and manifested forth his glory; and his disciples believed on him. After this he went down to Capernaum, he, and his mother, and his brethren, and his disciples: and they continued there not many days.

And the Jews' passover was at hand, and Jesus went up to Jerusalem. Now when he was in Jerusalem at the passover, in the feast *day,* many believed on his name, when they saw the miracles which he did.

John 4: 1-3, 46-54

When therefore the Lord knew how the Pharisees had heard that Jesus made and baptized more disciples than John, (though Jesus himself baptized not, but his disciples,) he left Judæa, and departed again into Galilee.

12

So Jesus came again into Cana of Galilee, where he made the water wine. And there was a certain nobleman, whose son was sick at Capernaum. When he heard that Jesus was come out of Judæa into Galilee, he went unto him, and besought him that he would come down, and heal his son: for he was at the point of death.

Then said Jesus unto him, Except ye see signs and wonders, ye will not believe.

The nobleman saith unto him, Sir, come down ere my child die.

Jesus saith unto him, Go thy way; thy son liveth. And the man believed the word that Jesus had spoken unto him, and he went his way. And as he was now going down, his servants met him, and told *him,* saying, Thy son liveth.

Then enquired he of them the hour when he began to amend. And they said unto him, Yesterday at the seventh hour the fever left him.

So the father knew that *it was* at the same hour, in the which Jesus said unto him, Thy son liveth: and himself believed, and his whole house. This *is* again the second miracle *that* Jesus did, when he was come out of Judæa into Galilee.

After this there was a feast of the Jews; and Jesus went up to Jerusalem. John 5: 1-9

Now there is at Jerusalem by the sheep *market* a pool, which is called in the Hebrew tongue Bethesda, having five porches. In these lay a great multitude of impotent folk, of blind, halt, withered, waiting for the moving of the water. For an angel went down at a certain season into the pool, and troubled the water: whosoever then first after the troubling of the water stepped in was made whole of whatsoever disease he had.

And a certain man was there, which had an infirmity thirty and eight years. When Jesus saw him lie, and knew that he had been now a long time *in that case,* he saith unto him, Wilt thou be made whole?

The impotent man answered him, Sir, I have no man, when the water is troubled, to put me into the pool: but while I am coming, another steppeth down before me.

Jesus saith unto him, Rise, take up thy bed, and walk.

And immediately the man was made whole, and took up his bed, and walked: and on the same day was the sabbath.

Luke 4:
14, 31,
38, 39

And Jesus returned in the power of the Spirit into Galilee: and there went out a fame of him through all the region round about. And (he) came down to Capernaum, a city of Galilee, . . . and entered into Simon's house. And Simon's wife's mother was taken with a great fever; and they besought him for her. And he stood over her, and rebuked the fever; and it left her: and immediately she arose and ministered unto them.

Luke 6:
12-19

And it came to pass in those days, that (Jesus) went out into a mountain to pray, and continued all night in prayer to God. And when it was day, he called *unto him* his disciples: and of them he chose twelve, whom he also named apostles; Simon, (whom he also named Peter,) and Andrew his brother, James and John, Philip and Bartholomew, Matthew and Thomas, James the *son* of Alphæus, and Simon called Zelotes, and Judas *the brother* of James, and Judas Iscariot, which also was the traitor.

And he came down with them, and stood in the

plain, and the company of his disciples, and a great multitude of people out of all Judæa and Jerusalem, and from the sea coast of Tyre and Sidon, which came to hear him, and to be healed of their diseases; and they that were vexed with unclean spirits: and they were healed. And the whole multitude sought to touch him: for there went virtue out of him, and healed *them* all.

And a certain centurion's servant, who was dear unto him, was sick, and ready to die. And when he heard of Jesus, he sent unto him the elders of the Jews, beseeching him that he would come and heal his servant. And when they came to Jesus, they besought him instantly, saying, That he was worthy for whom he should do this: for he loveth our nation, and he hath built us a synagogue.

Luke 7: 2-10, 36-48, 50

Then Jesus went with them. And when he was now not far from the house, the centurion sent friends to him, saying unto him, Lord, trouble not thyself: for I am not worthy that thou shouldest enter under my roof: wherefore neither thought I myself worthy to come unto thee: but say in a word, and my servant shall be healed. For I also am a man set under authority, having under me soldiers, and I say unto one, Go, and he goeth; and to another, Come, and he cometh; and to my servant, Do this, and he doeth *it*.

When Jesus heard these things, he marvelled at him, and turned him about, and said unto the people that followed him, I say unto you, I have not found so great faith, no, not in Israel.

And they that were sent, returning to the house, found the servant whole that had been sick.

And one of the Pharisees desired him that he would eat with him. And he went into the Pharisee's house, and sat down to meat.

And, behold, a woman in the city, which was a sinner, when she knew that *Jesus* sat at meat in the Pharisee's house, brought an alabaster box of ointment, and stood at his feet behind *him* weeping, and began to wash his feet with tears, and did wipe *them* with the hairs of her head, and kissed his feet, and anointed *them* with the ointment.

Now when the Pharisee which had bidden him saw *it,* he spake within himself, saying, This man, if he were a prophet, would have known who and what manner of woman *this is* that toucheth him: for she is a sinner.

And Jesus answering said unto him, Simon, I have somewhat to say unto thee.

And he saith, Master, say on.

There was a certain creditor which had two debtors: the one owed five hundred pence, and the other fifty. And when they had nothing to pay, he frankly forgave them both. Tell me therefore, which of them will love him most?

Simon answered and said, I suppose that *he,* to whom he forgave most.

And (Jesus) said unto him, Thou hast rightly judged.

And he turned to the woman, and said unto Simon, Seest thou this woman? I entered into thine house, thou gavest me no water for my feet: but she hath washed my feet with tears, and wiped *them* with the hairs of her head. Thou gavest me no kiss: but this woman since the time I came in hath not ceased to kiss my feet. My head with oil thou didst not anoint: but this woman hath anointed my feet with ointment. Wherefore I say unto thee, Her sins, which are many, are forgiven; for she loved much: but to whom little is forgiven, *the same* loveth little.

And he said unto her, Thy sins are forgiven. . . . Thy faith hath saved thee; go in peace.

And, behold, there came a man named Jairus, and he was a ruler of the synagogue: and he fell down at Jesus' feet, and besought him that he would come into his house: for he had one only daughter, about twelve years of age, and she lay a dying. . . .

Luke 8: 41, 42, 49-55

. . . There cometh one from the ruler of the synagogue's *house,* saying to him, Thy daughter is dead; trouble not the Master.

But when Jesus heard *it,* he answered him, saying, Fear not: believe only, and she shall be made whole.

And when he came into the house, he suffered no man to go in, save Peter, and James, and John, and the father and the mother of the maiden.

And all wept, and bewailed her: but he said, Weep not; she is not dead, but sleepeth.

And they laughed him to scorn, knowing that she was dead. And he put them all out, and took her by the hand, and called, saying, Maid, arise.

And her spirit came again, and she arose straightway: and he commanded to give her meat.

And when Jesus departed thence, two blind men followed him, crying, and saying, *Thou* son of David, have mercy on us.

Matthew 9: 27-31

And when he was come into the house, the blind men came to him: and Jesus saith unto them, Believe ye that I am able to do this?

They said unto him, Yea, Lord.

Then touched he their eyes, saying, According to your faith be it unto you.

And their eyes were opened; and Jesus straitly charged them, saying, See *that* no man know *it.*

But they, when they were departed, spread abroad his fame in all that country.

Luke 9:
1, 2, 6,
10, 11 Then he called his twelve disciples together, and gave them power and authority over all devils, and to cure diseases. And he sent them to preach the kingdom of God, and to heal the sick. And they departed, and went through the towns, preaching the gospel, and healing every where.

And the apostles, when they were returned, told him all that they had done. And he took them, and went aside privately into a desert place. . . . And the people, when they knew *it,* followed him: and he received them, and spake unto them of the kingdom of God, and healed them that had need of healing.

Matthew 14:
22-33 And straightway Jesus constrained his disciples to get into a ship, and to go before him unto the other side, while he sent the multitudes away. And when he had sent the multitudes away, he went up into a mountain apart to pray: and when the evening was come, he was there alone. But the ship was now in the midst of the sea, tossed with waves: for the wind was contrary. And in the fourth watch of the night Jesus went unto them, walking on the sea.

And when the disciples saw him walking on the sea, they were troubled, saying, It is a spirit; and they cried out for fear.

But straightway Jesus spake unto them, saying, Be of good cheer; it is I; be not afraid.

And Peter answered him and said, Lord, if it be thou, bid me come unto thee on the water.

And he said, Come.

And when Peter was come down out of the ship, he walked on the water, to go to Jesus. But when he saw the wind boisterous, he was afraid; and beginning to sink, he cried, saying, Lord, save me.

And immediately Jesus stretched forth *his* hand, and caught him, and said unto him, O thou of little faith, wherefore didst thou doubt?

And when they were come into the ship, the wind ceased. Then they that were in the ship came and worshipped him, saying, Of a truth thou art the Son of God.

And Jesus . . . went up into a mountain, and sat down there (in Decapolis). And great multitudes came unto him, having with them *those that were* lame, blind, dumb, maimed, and many others, and cast them down at Jesus' feet; and he healed them: insomuch that the multitude wondered, when they saw the dumb to speak, the maimed to be whole, the lame to walk, and the blind to see: and they glorified the God of Israel.

Then Jesus called his disciples *unto him,* and said, I have compassion on the multitude, because they continue with me now three days, and have nothing to eat: and I will not send them away fasting, lest they faint in the way.

And his disciples say unto him, Whence should we have so much bread in the wilderness, as to fill so great a multitude?

And Jesus saith unto them, How many loaves have ye?

And they said, Seven, and a few little fishes.

And he commanded the multitude to sit down on the ground. And he took the seven loaves and the fishes, and gave thanks, and brake *them,* and gave to his disciples, and the disciples to the multitude. And they did all eat, and were filled: and they took up of the broken *meat* that was left seven baskets full.

Matthew 15: 29-39

And they that did eat were four thousand men, beside women and children.

And he sent away the multitude, and took ship, . . .

Matthew 16:
13-16, 20 When Jesus came into the coasts of Cæsarea Philippi, he asked his disciples, saying, Whom do men say that I the Son of man am?

And they said, Some *say that thou art* John the Baptist: some, Elias; and others, Jeremias, or one of the prophets.

He saith unto them, But whom say ye that I am?

And Simon Peter answered and said, Thou art the Christ, the Son of the living God.

Then charged he his disciples that they should tell no man that he was Jesus the Christ.

Matthew 17:
1-9, 14-21 And after six days Jesus taketh Peter, James, and John his brother, and bringeth them up into an high mountain apart, and was transfigured before them: and his face did shine as the sun, and his raiment was white as the light.

And, behold, there appeared unto them Moses and Elias talking with him.

Then answered Peter, and said unto Jesus, Lord, it is good for us to be here: if thou wilt, let us make here three tabernacles; one for thee, and one for Moses, and one for Elias.

While he yet spake, behold, a bright cloud overshadowed them: and behold a voice out of the cloud, which said, This is my beloved Son, in whom I am well pleased; hear ye him.

And when the disciples heard *it,* they fell on their face, and were sore afraid.

And Jesus came and touched them, and said, Arise, and be not afraid.

And when they had lifted up their eyes, they saw no man, save Jesus only. And as they came down from the mountain, Jesus charged them, saying, Tell the vision to no man, until the Son of man be risen again from the dead.

And when they were come to the multitude, there came to him a *certain* man, kneeling down to him, and saying, Lord, have mercy on my son: for he is lunatick, and sore vexed: for ofttimes he falleth into the fire, and oft into the water. And I brought him to thy disciples, and they could not cure him.

Then Jesus answered and said, O faithless and perverse generation, how long shall I be with you? how long shall I suffer you? bring him hither to me.

And Jesus rebuked the devil; and he departed out of him: and the child was cured from that very hour.

Then came the disciples to Jesus apart, and said, Why could not we cast him out?

And Jesus said unto them, Because of your unbelief: for verily I say unto you, If ye have faith as a grain of mustard seed, ye shall say unto this mountain, Remove hence to yonder place; and it shall remove; and nothing shall be impossible unto you. Howbeit this kind goeth not out but by prayer and fasting.

Now a certain *man* was sick, *named* Lazarus, of Bethany, the town of Mary and her sister Martha. John 11: 1, 4, 5, 20-27, 32-34, 38-46

When Jesus heard *that,* he said, This sickness is not unto death, but for the glory of God, that the Son of God might be glorified thereby.

Now Jesus loved Martha, and her sister, and Lazarus. Then Martha, as soon as she heard that Jesus was coming, went and met him: but Mary sat *still* in the house. Then said Martha unto Jesus, Lord, if thou hadst been here, my brother had not died. But I know, that even now, whatsoever thou wilt ask of God, God will give *it* thee.

Jesus saith unto her, Thy brother shall rise again.

Martha saith unto him, I know that he shall rise again in the resurrection at the last day.

Jesus said unto her, I am the resurrection, and the life: he that believeth in me, though he were dead, yet shall he live: and whosoever liveth and believeth in me shall never die. Believest thou this?

She saith unto him, Yea, Lord: I believe that thou art the Christ, the Son of God, which should come into the world.

Then when Mary was come where Jesus was, and saw him, she fell down at his feet, saying unto him, Lord, if thou hadst been here, my brother had not died.

When Jesus therefore saw her weeping, and the Jews also weeping which came with her, he groaned in the spirit, and was troubled, and said, Where have ye laid him?

They said unto him, Lord, come and see.

Jesus therefore again groaning in himself cometh to the grave. It was a cave, and a stone lay upon it.

Jesus said, Take ye away the stone. . . .

Martha . . . saith, . . . Lord, . . . he hath been *dead* four days.

Jesus saith unto her, Said I not unto thee, that, if thou wouldest believe, thou shouldest see the glory of God?

Then they took away the stone *from the place* where the dead was laid. And Jesus lifted up *his* eyes, and said, Father, I thank thee that thou hast heard me. And I knew that thou hearest me always: but because of the people which stand by I said *it,* that they may believe that thou hast sent me.

And when he thus had spoken, he cried with a loud voice, Lazarus, come forth.

And he that was dead came forth, bound hand and foot with graveclothes: and his face was bound about with a napkin.

Jesus saith unto them, Loose him, and let him go.

Then many of the Jews which came to Mary, and had seen the things which Jesus did, believed on him. But some of them went their ways to the Pharisees, and told them what things Jesus had done.

Some of Jesus' Teachings and Parables

PROPHESY: Isaiah 55:1 Ho, every one that thirsteth, come ye to the waters, and he that hath no money; come ye, buy, and eat; yea, come, buy wine and milk without money and without price.

Isaiah 52:7 How beautiful upon the mountains are the feet of him that bringeth good tidings, that publisheth peace; that bringeth good tidings of good, that publisheth salvation; that saith unto Zion, Thy God reigneth!

Isaiah 55:3, 4 Incline your ear, and come unto me: hear, and your soul shall live; . . . Behold, I have given him *for* a witness to the people, a leader and commander to the people.

Psalms 78:2 I will open my mouth in a parable: . . .

Luke 4: 16-22

AND (Jesus) came to Nazareth, where he had been brought up: and, as his custom was, he went into the synagogue on the sabbath day, and stood up . . . to read. And there was delivered unto him the book of the prophet Esaias. And when he had opened the book, he found the place where it was written, The Spirit of the Lord *is* upon me, because he hath anointed me to preach the gospel to the poor; he hath sent me to heal the brokenhearted, to preach deliverance to the captives, and recovering of sight to the blind, to set at liberty them that are bruised, to preach the acceptable year of the Lord.

24

And he closed the book, and he gave *it* again to the minister, and sat down. And the eyes of all them that were in the synagogue were fastened on him.

And he began to say unto them, This day is this scripture fulfilled in your ears.

And all bear him witness, and wondered at the gracious words which proceeded out of his mouth. . . .

Now about the midst of the feast Jesus went up into the temple, and taught. And the Jews marvelled, saying, How knoweth this man letters, having never learned?

John 7: 14-17

Jesus answered them, and said, My doctrine is not mine, but his that sent me. If any man will do his will, he shall know of the doctrine, whether it be of God, or *whether* I speak of myself.

And seeing the multitudes, he went up into a mountain: and when he was set, his disciples came unto him: and he opened his mouth, and taught them, saying,

Matthew 5: 1-12

Blessed *are* the poor in spirit: for their's is the kingdom of heaven.

Blessed *are* they that mourn: for they shall be comforted.

Blessed *are* the meek: for they shall inherit the earth.

Blessed *are* they which do hunger and thirst after righteousness: for they shall be filled.

Blessed *are* the merciful: for they shall obtain mercy.

Blessed *are* the pure in heart: for they shall see God.

Blessed *are* the peacemakers: for they shall be called the children of God.

Blessed *are* they which are persecuted for righteousness' sake: for their's is the kingdom of heaven.

Blessed are ye, when *men* shall revile you, and persecute *you,* and shall say all manner of evil against you falsely, for my sake. Rejoice, and be exceeding glad: for great *is* your reward in heaven: for so persecuted they the prophets which were before you.

Luke 6: 27,28 — But I say unto you which hear, Love your enemies, do good to them which hate you, bless them that curse you, and pray for them which despitefully use you.

Matthew 18: 21, 22 15, 16 — Then came Peter to him, and said, Lord, how oft shall my brother sin against me, and I forgive him? till seven times?

Jesus saith unto him, I say not unto thee, Until seven times: but, Until seventy times seven.

Moreover if thy brother shall trespass against thee, go and tell him his fault between thee and him alone: if he shall hear thee, thou hast gained thy brother. But if he will not hear *thee, then* take with thee one or two more, that in the mouth of two or three witnesses every word may be established.

Matthew 5: 17, 18 — Think not that I am come to destroy the law, or the prophets: I am not come to destroy, but to fulfil. For verily I say unto you, Till heaven and earth pass, one jot or one tittle shall in no wise pass from the law, till all be fulfilled.

Luke 10: 25-37 — And, behold, a certain lawyer stood up, and tempted him, saying, Master, what shall I do to inherit eternal life?

He said unto him, What is written in the law? how readest thou?

And he answering said, Thou shalt love the Lord thy God with all thy heart, and with all thy soul, and with all thy strength, and with all thy mind; and thy neighbour as thyself.

And he said unto him, Thou hast answered right: this do, and thou shalt live.

But he, willing to justify himself, said unto Jesus, And who is my neighbour?

And Jesus answering said, A certain *man* went down from Jerusalem to Jericho, and fell among thieves, which stripped him of his raiment, and wounded *him,* and departed, leaving *him* half dead. And by chance there came down a certain priest that way: and when he saw him, he passed by on the other side. And likewise a Levite, when he was at the place, came and looked *on him,* and passed by on the other side.

But a certain Samaritan, as he journeyed, came where he was: and when he saw him, he had compassion *on him,* and went to *him,* and bound up his wounds, pouring in oil and wine, and set him on his own beast, and brought him to an inn, and took care of him. And on the morrow when he departed, he took out two pence, and gave *them* to the host, and said unto him, Take care of him; and whatsoever thou spendest more, when I come again, I will repay thee.

Which now of these three, thinkest thou, was neighbour unto him that fell among the thieves?

And he said, He that shewed mercy on him.

Then said Jesus unto him, Go, and do thou likewise.

Give to every man that asketh of thee; and of him that taketh away thy goods ask *them* not again. And as ye would that men should do to you, do ye also to them likewise.

Luke 6: 30, 31, 33, 38

And if ye do good to them which do good to you, what thank have ye? for sinners also do even the same.

Give, and it shall be given unto you; good measure, pressed down, and shaken together, and running over, shall men give into your bosom. For with the same measure that ye mete withal it shall be measured to you again.

Luke 11: 9, 11, 13 And I say unto you, Ask, and it shall be given you; seek, and ye shall find; knock, and it shall be opened unto you.

If a son shall ask bread of any of you that is a father, will he give him a stone? . . . If ye then, being evil, know how to give good gifts unto your children: how much more shall *your* heavenly Father give the Holy Spirit to them that ask him?

Luke 12: 15-24, 27, 31, 32 And he said unto them, Take heed, and beware of covetousness: for a man's life consisteth not in the abundance of the things which he possesseth.

And he spake a parable unto them, saying, The ground of a certain rich man brought forth plentifully: and he thought within himself, saying, What shall I do, because I have no room where to bestow my fruits?

And he said, This will I do: I will pull down my barns, and build greater; and there will I bestow all my fruits and my goods. And I will say to my soul, Soul, thou hast much goods laid up for many years; take thine ease, eat, drink, *and* be merry.

But God said unto him, *Thou* fool, this night thy soul shall be required of thee: then whose shall those things be, which thou hast provided?

So *is* he that layeth up treasure for himself, and is not rich toward God.

And (Jesus) said unto his disciples, Therefore I say unto you, Take no thought for your life, what ye shall eat; neither for the body, what ye shall put on. The life is more than meat, and the body *is more* than raiment. Consider the ravens: for they neither sow nor reap; which neither have storehouse nor barn; and God feedeth them: how much more are ye better than the fowls? Consider the lilies how they grow: they toil not, they spin not; and yet I say unto you, that Solomon in all his glory was not arrayed like one of these.

But rather seek ye the kingdom of God; and all these things shall be added unto you. Fear not, little flock; for it is your Father's good pleasure to give you the kingdom.

. . . One of his disciples said unto him, Lord, teach us to pray, . . . Luke 11: 1

(Jesus saith) . . . When thou prayest, enter into thy closet, and when thou hast shut thy door, pray to thy Father which is in secret; and thy Father which seeth in secret shall reward thee openly. But when ye pray, use not vain repetitions, as the heathen *do*: for they think that they shall be heard for their much speaking. Matthew 6: 6, 7, 9-13

After this manner therefore pray ye: Our Father which art in heaven, Hallowed be thy name. Thy kingdom come. Thy will be done in earth, as *it is* in heaven. Give us this day our daily bread. And forgive us our debts, as we forgive our debtors. And lead us not into temptation, but deliver us from evil: For thine is the kingdom, and the power, and the glory, for ever. Amen.

And they brought young children to him, that he should touch them: and *his* disciples rebuked those that brought *them*. But when Jesus saw *it,* he was much displeased, and said unto them, Suffer the little children to come unto me, and forbid them not: for of such is the kingdom of God. Verily I say unto you, Mark 10: 13-15

Whosoever shall not receive the kingdom of God as a little child, he shall not enter therein.

Matthew 18:
1-4

At the same time came the disciples unto Jesus, saying, Who is the greatest in the kingdom of heaven?

And Jesus called a little child unto him, and set him in the midst of them, and said, Verily I say unto you, Except ye be converted, and become as little children, ye shall not enter into the kingdom of heaven. Whosoever therefore shall humble himself as this little child, the same is greatest in the kingdom of heaven.

Matthew 13:
44-46

. . . The kingdom of heaven is like unto treasure hid in a field; the which when a man hath found, he hideth, and for joy thereof goeth and selleth all that he hath, and buyeth that field.

Again, the kingdom of heaven is like unto a merchant man, seeking goodly pearls: who, when he had found one pearl of great price, went and sold all that he had, and bought it.

Matthew 25:
1-13

Then shall the kingdom of heaven be likened unto ten virgins, which took their lamps, and went forth to meet the bridegroom. And five of them were wise, and five *were* foolish. They that *were* foolish took their lamps, and took no oil with them: but the wise took oil in their vessels with their lamps.

While the bridegroom tarried, they all slumbered and slept. And at midnight there was a cry made, Behold, the bridegroom cometh; go ye out to meet him.

Then all those virgins arose, and trimmed their lamps.

And the foolish said unto the wise, Give us of your oil; for our lamps are gone out.

But the wise answered, saying, *Not so;* lest there be not enough for us and you: but go . . . to them that sell, and buy for yourselves.

And while they went to buy, the bridegroom came; and they that were ready went in with him to the marriage: and the door was shut.

Afterward came also the other virgins, saying, Lord, Lord, open to us.

But he answered and said, Verily I say unto you, I know you not.

Watch therefore, for ye know neither the day nor the hour wherein the Son of man cometh.

. . . When the Son of man cometh, shall he find faith on the earth? *Luke 18: 8*

And why call ye me, Lord, Lord, and do not the things which I say? *Luke 6: 46-49*

Whosoever cometh to me, and heareth my sayings, and doeth them, I will shew you to whom he is like: he is like a man which built an house, and digged deep, and laid the foundation on a rock: and when the flood arose, the stream beat vehemently upon that house, and could not shake it: for it was founded upon a rock. But he that heareth, and doeth not, is like a man that without a foundation built an house upon the earth; against which the stream did beat vehemently, and immediately it fell; and the ruin of that house was great.

No servant can serve two masters: for either he will hate the one, and love the other; or else he will hold to the one, and despise the other. Ye cannot serve God and mammon. *Luke 16: 13*

Come unto me, all *ye* that labour and are heavy laden, and I will give you rest. Take my yoke upon you, and learn of me; for I am meek and lowly in heart: and ye shall find rest unto your souls. For my yoke *is* easy, and my burden is light. *Matthew 11: 28-30*

John 10:
14, 15
I am the good shepherd, and know my *sheep,* and am known of mine. As the Father knoweth me, even so know I the Father: and I lay down my life for the sheep.

Luke 15:
1-7,
11-24
Then drew near unto him all the publicans and sinners . . . to hear him. And the Pharisees and scribes murmured, saying, This man receiveth sinners, and eateth with them.

And he spake this parable unto them, saying, What man of you, having an hundred sheep, if he lose one of them, doth not leave the ninety and nine in the wilderness, and go after that which is lost, until he find it? and when he hath found *it,* he layeth *it* on his shoulders, rejoicing. And when he cometh home, he calleth together *his* friends and neighbours, saying unto them, Rejoice with me; for I have found my sheep which was lost.

I say unto you, that likewise joy shall be in heaven over one sinner that repenteth, more than over ninety and nine just persons, which need no repentance.

And he said, A certain man had two sons: and the younger of them said to *his* father, Father, give me the portion of goods that falleth *to me.*

And he divided unto them *his* living.

And not many days after the younger son gathered all together, and took his journey into a far country, and there wasted his substance with riotous living. And when he had spent all, there arose a mighty famine in that land; and he began to be in want. And he went and joined himself to a citizen of that country; and he sent him into his fields to feed swine. And he would fain have filled his belly with the husks that the swine did eat: and no man gave unto him.

And when he came to himself, he said, How many

hired servants of my father's have bread enough and to spare, and I perish with hunger! I will arise and go to my father, and will say unto him, Father, I have sinned against heaven, and before thee, and am no more worthy to be called thy son: make me as one of thy hired servants.

And he arose, and came to his father. But when he was yet a great way off, his father saw him, and had compassion, and ran, and fell on his neck, and kissed him.

And the son said unto him, Father, I have sinned against heaven, and in thy sight, and am no more worthy to be called thy son.

But the father said to his servants, Bring forth the best robe, and put *it* on him; and put a ring on his hand, and shoes on *his* feet: and bring hither the fatted calf, and kill *it;* and let us eat, and be merry: for this my son was dead, and is alive again; he was lost and is found. . . .

And (Jesus) spake this parable unto certain which trusted in themselves that they were righteous, and despised others: Luke 18: 9-14

Two men went up into the temple to pray; the one a Pharisee, and the other a publican. The Pharisee stood and prayed thus with himself, God, I thank thee, that I am not as other men *are,* extortioners, unjust, adulterers, or even as this publican. I fast twice in the week, I give tithes of all that I possess.

And the publican, standing afar off, would not lift up so much as *his* eyes unto heaven, but smote upon his breast, saying, God be merciful to me a sinner.

I tell you, this man went down to his house justified *rather* than the other: for every one that exalteth himself shall be abased; and he that humbleth himself shall be exalted.

Luke 6: 41

And why beholdest thou the mote that *is* in thy brother's eye, but perceivest not the beam that *is* in thine own eye?

Luke 11: 42, 43, 53, 54

. . . Woe unto you, Pharisees! for ye tithe mint and rue and all manner of herbs, and pass over judgment and the love of God: these ought ye to have done, and not to leave the other undone. Woe unto you, Pharisees! for ye love the uppermost seats in the synagogues, and greetings in the markets.

And as he said these things unto them, the scribes and the Pharisees began to urge *him* vehemently, and to provoke him to speak of many things: laying wait for him, and seeking to catch something out of his mouth, that they might accuse him.

Luke 12: 1, 2

In the mean time, when there were gathered together an innumerable multitude of people, . . . he began to say unto his disciples first of all, Beware ye of the leaven of the Pharisees, which is hypocrisy. For there is nothing covered, that shall not be revealed; neither hid, that shall not be known.

Luke 21: 8-11, 26, 28

And he said, Take heed that ye be not deceived: for many shall come in my name, saying, I am *Christ;* . . . go ye not therefore after them.

But when ye shall hear of wars and commotions, be not terrified: for these things must first come to pass; but the end *is* not by and by.

Then said he unto them, Nation shall rise against nation, and kingdom against kingdom: and great earthquakes shall be in divers places, and famines, and pestilences; and fearful sights and great signs shall there be from heaven. Men's hearts failing them for fear, and for looking after those things which are coming on the earth: for the powers of heaven shall be shaken. And when these things begin to come to pass, then look up, and lift up your heads; for your redemption draweth nigh.

Let not your heart be troubled: ye believe in God, believe also in me. In my Father's house are many mansions: if *it were* not *so,* I would have told you. I go to prepare a place for you. And if I go and prepare a place for you, I will come again, and receive you unto myself; that where I am, *there* ye may be also. And whither I go ye know, and the way ye know.

John 14:
1-12,
15-17,
26-27

Thomas saith unto him, Lord, we know not whither thou goest; and how can we know the way?

Jesus saith unto him, I am the way, the truth, and the life: no man cometh unto the Father, but by me. If ye had known me, ye should have known my Father also: and from henceforth ye know him, and have seen him.

Philip saith unto him, Lord, shew us the Father, and it sufficeth us.

Jesus saith unto him, Have I been so long time with you, and yet hast thou not known me, Philip? he that hath seen me hath seen the Father; and how sayest thou *then,* Shew us the Father? believest thou not that I am in the Father, and the Father in me? the words that I speak unto you I speak not of myself: but the Father that dwelleth in me, he doeth the works. Believe me that I *am* in the Father, and the Father in me: or else believe me for the very works' sake. Verily, verily, I say unto you, He that believeth on me, the works that I do shall he do also; and greater *works* than these shall he do; because I go unto my Father.

If ye love me, keep my commandments.

And I will pray the Father, and he shall give you another Comforter, that he may abide with you for ever; *even* the Spirit of truth; whom the world cannot receive, because it seeth him not, neither knoweth him: ... But the Comforter, *which is* the Holy Ghost, whom the Father will send in my name, he shall teach you all things, and bring all things to your remembrance, whatsoever I have said unto you.

Peace I leave with you, my peace I give unto you: not as the world giveth, give I unto you. Let not your heart be troubled, neither let it be afraid.

Matthew 24: 35 Heaven and earth shall pass away, but my words shall not pass away.*

*See explanation of this Chapter in Preface.

Resistance to Jesus and His Protection

PROPHESY: Isaiah 53:3 He is despised and rejected of men; a man of sorrows, and acquainted with grief: and we hid as it were *our* faces from him; he was despised, and we esteemed him not.

Isaiah 54:17 No weapon that is formed against thee shall prosper; and every tongue *that* shall rise against thee in judgment thou shalt condemn. . . .

AND when the sabbath day was come, he began to teach in the synagogue: and many hearing *him* were astonished, saying, From whence hath this *man* these things? and what wisdom *is* this which is given unto him, that even such mighty works are wrought by his hands? Is not this the carpenter, the son of Mary, the brother of James, and Joses, and of Juda, and Simon? and are not his sisters here with us? Mark 6: 2-6

And they were offended at him.

But Jesus said unto them, A prophet is not without honour, but in his own country, and among his own kin, and in his own house.

And he could there do no mighty work, save that he laid his hands upon a few sick folk, and healed *them*. And he marvelled because of their unbelief. . . .

And he said, . . . I tell you of a truth, many widows were in Israel in the days of Elias, when the heaven was shut up three years and six months, when great Luke 4: 24-30

37

THE LIFE OF CHRIST JESUS

famine was throughout all the land; but unto none of them was Elias sent, save unto Sarepta, *a city* of Sidon, unto a woman *that was* a widow. And many lepers were in Israel in the time of Eliseus the prophet; and none of them was cleansed, saving Naaman the Syrian.

And all they in the synagogue, when they heard these things, were filled with wrath, and rose up, and thrust him out of the city, and led him unto the brow of the hill whereon their city was built, that they might cast him down headlong. But he passing through the midst of them went his way.

Luke 5:
17-25

And it came to pass on a certain day, as he was teaching, . . . behold, men brought in a bed a man which was taken with a palsy: . . . And when they could not find by what *way* they might bring him in because of the multitude, they went upon the housetop, and let him down through the tiling with *his* couch into the midst before Jesus.

And when he saw their faith, he said unto him, Man, thy sins are forgiven thee.

And the scribes and the Pharisees began to reason, saying, Who is this which speaketh blasphemies? Who can forgive sins, but God alone?

But when Jesus perceived their thoughts, he answering said unto them, What reason ye in your hearts? Whether is easier, to say, Thy sins be forgiven thee; or to say, Rise up and walk?

But that ye may know that the Son of man hath power upon earth to forgive sins, (he said unto the sick of the palsy,) I say unto thee, Arise, and take up thy couch, and go into thine house.

And immediately he rose up before them, and took up that whereon he lay, and departed to his own house, glorifying God.

And it came to pass also on another sabbath, that he entered into the synagogue and taught: and there was a man whose right hand was withered. And the scribes and Pharisees watched him, whether he would heal on the sabbath day; that they might find an accusation against him. But he knew their thoughts, and said to the man which had the withered hand, Rise up, and stand forth in the midst. Luke 6: 6-11

And he arose and stood forth.

Then said Jesus unto them, I will ask you one thing; Is it lawful on the sabbath days to do good, or to do evil? to save life, or to destroy *it?*

And looking round about upon them all, he said unto the man, Stretch forth thy hand.

And he did so: and his hand was restored whole as the other.

And they were filled with madness; and communed one with another what they might do to Jesus.

After these things Jesus walked in Galilee: for he would not walk in Jewry, because the Jews sought to kill him. John 7: 1, 2, 14, 30, 32, 45, 46

Now the Jews' feast of tabernacles was at hand (at Jerusalem). Now about the midst of the feast Jesus went up into the temple, and taught. Then they sought to take him: but no man laid hands on him, because his hour was not yet come. . . . And the Pharisees and the chief priests sent officers to take him. Then came the officers to the chief priests and Pharisees; and they said unto them, Why have ye not brought him?

The officers answered, Never man spake like this man.

John 8:
1, 2,
12-15,
46, 51,
52, 58, 59 Jesus went unto the mount of Olives. And early in the morning he came again into the temple, and all the people came unto him; and he sat down, and taught them.

Then spake Jesus again unto them, saying, I am the light of the world: he that followeth me shall not walk in darkness, but shall have the light of life.

The Pharisees therefore said unto him, Thou bearest record of thyself; thy record is not true.

Jesus answered and said unto them, Though I bear record of myself, *yet* my record is true: for I know whence I came, and whither I go; but ye cannot tell whence I come, and whither I go. Ye judge after the flesh; I judge no man. Which of you convinceth me of sin? And if I say the truth, why do ye not believe me? Verily, verily, I say unto you, If a man keep my saying, he shall never see death.

Then said the Jews unto him, Now we know that thou hast a devil. Abraham is dead, and the prophets; and thou sayest, If a man keep my saying, he shall never taste of death.

Jesus said unto them, Verily, verily, I say unto you, Before Abraham was, I am.

Then took they . . . stones to cast at him: but Jesus hid himself, and went out of the temple, going through the midst of them, and so passed by.

John 11:
47, 48,
53 Then gathered the chief priests and the Pharisees a council, and said, What do we? for this man doeth many miracles. If we let him thus alone, all *men* will believe on him: . . . Then from that day forth they took counsel together . . . to put him to death.

Betrayal and Crucifixion

PROPHESY: Isaiah 59:7 Their feet run to evil, and they make haste to shed innocent blood: . . .

Isaiah 53:7 He was oppressed, and he was afflicted, yet he opened not his mouth: he is brought as a lamb to the slaughter, and as a sheep before her shearers is dumb, so he openeth not his mouth.

Isaiah 54:7 For a small moment have I forsaken thee; but with great mercies will I gather thee.

Matthew 20:17-19 And Jesus going up to Jerusalem took the twelve disciples apart in the way, and said unto them, Behold, we go up to Jerusalem; and the Son of man shall be betrayed unto the chief priests and unto the scribes, and they shall condemn him to death, and shall deliver him to the Gentiles to mock, and to scourge, and to crucify *him*: . . .

THEN assembled together the chief priests, and the scribes, and the elders of the people, unto the palace of the high priest, who was called Caiaphas, and consulted that they might take Jesus by subtilty, and kill *him*.

Matthew 26: 3-5, 14-16

But they said, Not on the feast *day*, lest there be an uproar among the people.

Then one of the twelve, called Judas Iscariot, went unto the chief priests, and said *unto them*, What will ye give me, and I will deliver him unto you?

And they covenanted with him for thirty pieces of silver. And from that time he sought opportunity to betray him.

Luke 22:
7, 14-16

Then came the day of unleavened bread, when the passover must be killed. And when the hour was come, he sat down, and the twelve apostles with him.

And he said unto them, With desire I have desired to eat this passover with you before I suffer: for I say unto you, I will not any more eat thereof, until it be fulfilled in the kingdom of God.

Matthew 26:
21-28

And as they did eat, he said, Verily I say unto you, that one of you shall betray me.

And they were exceeding sorrowful, and began every one of them to say unto him, Lord, is it I?

And he answered and said, He that dippeth *his* hand with me in the dish, the same shall betray me. The Son of man goeth as it is written of him: but woe unto that man by whom the Son of man is betrayed! ...

Then Judas, which betrayed him, answered and said, Master, is it I?

He said unto him, Thou hast said.

And as they were eating, Jesus took bread, and blessed *it,* and brake *it,* and gave *it* to the disciples, and said, Take, eat; this is my body.

And he took the cup, and gave thanks, and gave *it* to them, saying, Drink ye all of it; for this is my blood of the new testament, which is shed for many for the remission of sins.

John 13:
34, 35

A new commandment I give unto you, That ye love one another; as I have loved you, that ye also love one another. By this shall all *men* know that ye are my disciples, if ye have love one to another.

John 17:
1-5,
11, 15,
20, 21, 23

These words spake Jesus, and lifted up his eyes to heaven, and said, Father, the hour is come; glorify thy Son, that thy Son also may glorify thee: as thou hast given him power over all flesh, that he should give eternal life to as many as thou hast given him. And this is life eternal, that they might know thee the only true God, and Jesus Christ, whom thou hast sent.

I have glorified thee on the earth: I have finished the work which thou gavest me to do. And now, O Father, glorify thou me with thine own self with the glory which I had with thee before the world was.

And now I am no more in the world, but these are in the world, and I come to thee. Holy Father, keep through thine own name those whom thou hast given me, that they may be one, as we *are*. I pray not that thou shouldest take them out of the world, but that thou shouldest keep them from the evil. Neither pray I for these alone, but for them also which shall believe on me through their word; that they all may be one; as thou, Father, *art* in me, and I in thee, that they also may be one in us: that the world may believe that thou hast sent me. I in them, and thou in me, that they may be made perfect in one; and that the world may know that thou hast sent me, and hast loved them, as thou hast loved me.

And when they had sung an hymn, they went out into the mount of Olives. Matthew 26: 30-32, 36-42

Then saith Jesus unto them, All ye shall be offended because of me this night: for it is written, I will smite the shepherd, and the sheep of the flock shall be scattered abroad. But after I am risen again, I will go before you into Galilee.

Then cometh Jesus with them unto a place called Gethsemane, and saith unto the disciples, Sit ye here, while I go and pray yonder.

And he took with him Peter and the two sons of Zebedee, and began to be sorrowful and very heavy.

Then saith he unto them, My soul is exceeding sorrowful, even unto death: tarry ye here, and watch with me.

And he went a little farther, and fell on his face, and prayed, saying, O my Father, if it be possible, let this cup pass from me: nevertheless not as I will, but as thou *wilt*.

And he cometh unto the disciples, and findeth them asleep, and saith unto Peter, What, could ye not watch with me one hour? Watch and pray, that ye enter not into temptation: the spirit indeed *is* willing, but the flesh *is* weak.

He went away again the second time, and prayed, saying, O my Father, if this cup may not pass away from me, except I drink it, thy will be done.

Luke 22:
43

And there appeared an angel unto him from heaven, strengthening him.

Matthew 26:
43-45

And he came and found them asleep again: for their eyes were heavy. And he left them, and went away again, and prayed the third time, saying the same words.

Then cometh he to his disciples, and saith unto them, Sleep on now, and take *your* rest: behold, the hour is at hand, and the Son of man is betrayed into the hands of sinners.

Luke 22:
47, 48,
54, 66,
67, 70,
71

And while he yet spake, behold a multitude, and he that was called Judas, one of the twelve, went before them, and drew near unto Jesus to kiss him.

But Jesus said unto him, Judas, betrayest thou the Son of man with a kiss?

44

Then took they him, and led *him,* and brought him into the high priest's house. .... And as soon as it was day, the elders of the people and the chief priests and the scribes came together, and led him into their council, saying, Art thou the Christ? tell us.

And he said unto them, If I tell you, ye will not believe:

Then said they all, Art thou then the son of God?

And he said unto them, Ye say that I am.

And they said, What need we any further witness? for we ourselves have heard of his own mouth.

And the whole multitude of them arose, and led him unto Pilate. And they began to accuse him, saying, We found this *fellow* perverting the nation, and forbidding to give tribute to Cæsar, saying that he himself is Christ a King. Luke 23: 1-3

And Pilate asked him, saying, Art thou the King of the Jews? ...

Jesus answered him, Sayest thou this of thyself, or did others tell it thee of me? John 18: 34-37

Pilate answered, Am I a Jew? Thine own nation and the chief priests have delivered thee unto me: what hast thou done?

Jesus answered, My kingdom is not of this world; if my kingdom were of this world, then would my servants fight, that I should not be delivered to the Jews: ...

Pilate therefore said unto him, Art thou a king then?

Jesus answered, Thou sayest that I am a king. To this end was I born, and for this cause came I into the world, that I should bear witness unto the truth. ....

Then said Pilate to the chief priests and *to* the Luke 23: 4

45

Matthew 27: people, I find no fault in this man. For he knew that
18   for envy they had delivered him.

Luke 23:   And they were the more fierce, saying, He stirreth
5, 13-16, up the people, ...
21, 24

    And Pilate, when he had called together the chief
priests and the rulers and the people, said unto them,
Ye have brought this man unto me, as one that per-
verteth the people: and, behold, I, having examined
him before you, have found no fault in this man
touching those things whereof ye accuse him: no, nor
yet Herod: for I sent you to him; and, lo, nothing
worthy of death is done unto him. I will therefore
chastise him and release *him.*

    But they cried, saying, Crucify *him,* crucify him.

    And Pilate gave sentence that it should be as they
required.

John 19:   Then Pilate therefore took Jesus, and scourged
1-3, 5-12, *him.* And the soldiers platted a crown of thorns, and
16, 17 put *it* on his head, and they put on him a purple robe,
and said, Hail, King of the Jews! and they smote him
with their hands.

    Then came Jesus forth, wearing the crown of
thorns, and the purple robe. And *Pilate* saith unto
them, Behold the man!

    When the chief priests therefore and officers saw
him, they cried out, saying, Crucify *him,* crucify *him.*

    Pilate saith unto them, Take ye him, and crucify
him : for I find no fault in him.

    The Jews answered him, We have a law, and by
our law he ought to die, because he made himself the
Son of God.

    When Pilate therefore heard that saying, he was the
more afraid; and went again into the judgment hall,
and saith unto Jesus, Whence art thou?

But Jesus gave him no answer.

Then saith Pilate unto him, Speakest thou not unto me? knowest thou not that I have power to crucify thee, and have power to release thee?

Jesus answered, Thou couldest have no power *at all* against me, except it were given thee from above: . . .

And from thenceforth Pilate sought to release him: but the Jews cried out, saying, If thou let this man go, thou art not Cæsar's friend: whosoever maketh himself a king speaketh against Cæsar.

Then delivered he him therefore unto them to be crucified. And they took Jesus and led *him* away. And he bearing his cross went forth into a place called *the place* of a scull, which is called in the Hebrew Golgotha.

And when they were come to the place, which is called Calvary (scull), there they crucified him, and the malefactors, one on the right hand, and the other on the left. Luke 23: 33, 34, 44-46

Then said Jesus, Father, forgive them; for they know not what they do. . . .

And it was about the sixth hour, and there was a darkness over all the earth until the ninth hour. And the sun was darkened, and the veil of the temple was rent in the midst.

And when Jesus had cried with a loud voice, he said, Father, into thy hands I commend my spirit: and having said thus, he gave up the ghost.

When the even was come, there came a rich man of Arimathæa, named Joseph, who also himself was Jesus' disciple: he went to Pilate, and begged the body of Jesus. Then Pilate commanded the body to be delivered. And when Joseph had taken the body, he wrapped it in a clean linen cloth, and laid it in his own Matthew 27: 57-66 new tomb, which he had hewn out in the rock: and he rolled a great stone to the door of the sepulchre, and departed. And there was Mary Magdalene, and the other Mary, sitting over against the sepulchre.

Now the next day, that followed the day of the preparation, the chief priests and Pharisees came together unto Pilate, saying, Sir, we remember that that deceiver said, while he was yet alive, After three days I will rise again.

Command therefore that the sepulchre be made sure until the third day, lest his disciples come by night, and steal him away, and say unto the people, He is risen from the dead: so that the last error shall be worse than the first.

Pilate said unto them, Ye have a watch: go your way, make *it* as sure as ye can.

So they went, and made the sepulchre sure, sealing the stone, and setting a watch.

Resurrection and Ascension

PROPHESY: Isaiah 60:1, 3 Arise, shine; for thy light is come, and the glory of the Lord is risen upon thee. And the Gentiles shall come to thy light, and kings to the brightness of thy rising.

Isaiah 25:8 He will swallow up death in victory; ...

⟋⟋⟋⟋⟋

T HE first *day* of the week cometh Mary Magdalene early, when it was yet dark, unto the sepulchre, ... And, behold, there was a great earthquake: for the angel of the Lord descended from heaven, and came and rolled back the stone from the door, and sat upon it. And for fear of him the keepers did shake, and became as dead *men*. And the angel ... said ..., I know that ye seek Jesus, ... he is not here: for he is risen, ... John 20: 1 Matthew 28: 2, 4, 5, 6

Then (Mary) runneth, and cometh to Simon Peter, and to the other disciple, whom Jesus loved, and saith, ... They have taken away the Lord out of the sepulchre, and we know not where they have laid him. John 20: 2-17

Peter therefore went forth, and that other disciple, and came to the sepulchre. So they ran both together: and the other disciple did outrun Peter, and came first to the sepulchre. And he stooping down, *and looking in,* saw the linen clothes lying; yet went he not in.

Then cometh Simon Peter following him, and went into the sepulchre, and seeth the linen clothes lie, and the napkin, that was about his head, not lying with the linen clothes, but wrapped together in a place by itself. Then went in also that other disciple, which came first to the sepulchre, and he saw, and believed. For as yet they knew not the scripture, that he must rise again from the dead.

Then the disciples went away again unto their own home. But Mary stood without at the sepulchre weeping: and as she wept, she stooped down, *and looked* into the sepulchre, and seeth two angels in white sitting, the one at the head, and the other at the feet, where the body of Jesus had lain.

And they said unto her, Woman, why weepest thou?

She saith unto them, Because they have taken away my Lord, and I know not where they have laid him.

And when she had thus said, she turned herself back, and saw Jesus standing, and knew not that it was Jesus.

Jesus saith unto her, Woman, why weepest thou? whom seekest thou?

She, supposing him to be the gardener, saith unto him, Sir, if thou have borne him hence, tell me where thou hast laid him, and I will take him away.

Jesus saith unto her, Mary.

She turned herself, and saith unto him, Rabboni; which is to say, Master.

Jesus saith unto her, Touch me not; for I am not yet ascended to my Father: but go to my brethren, and say unto them, I ascend unto my Father, and your Father; and *to* my God, and your God.

Luke 24: 13-17, 27-43

And, behold, two of them went that same day to a village called Emmaus, which was from Jerusalem *about* threescore furlongs. And they talked together of all these things which had happened. And it came to pass, that, while they communed *together* and reasoned, Jesus himself drew near, and went with them. But their eyes were holden that they should not know him.

And he said unto them, What manner of communications *are* these that ye have one to another, as ye walk, and are sad?

And beginning at Moses and all the prophets, he expounded unto them in all the scriptures the things concerning himself. And they drew nigh unto the village, whither they went: and he made as though he would have gone further. But they constrained him, saying, Abide with us: for it is toward evening, and the day is far spent.

And he went in to tarry with them.

And it came to pass, as he sat at meat with them, he took bread, and blessed *it,* and brake, and gave to them. And their eyes were opened, and they knew him; and he vanished out of their sight.

And they said one to another, Did not our heart burn within us, while he talked with us by the way, and while he opened to us the scriptures?

And they rose up the same hour, and returned to Jerusalem, and found the eleven gathered together, and them that were with them, saying, The Lord is risen indeed, and hath appeared to Simon.

And they told what things *were done* in the way, and how he was known of them in breaking of bread. And as they thus spake, Jesus himself stood in the midst of them, and saith unto them, Peace *be* unto you.

But they were terrified and affrighted, and supposed that they had seen a spirit.

And he said unto them, Why are ye troubled? and why do thoughts arise in your hearts? Behold my hands and my feet, that it is I myself: handle me, and see; for a spirit hath not flesh and bones, as ye see me have.

And when he had thus spoken, he shewed them *his* hands and *his* feet.

And while they yet believed not for joy, and wondered, he said unto them, Have ye here any meat?

And they gave him a piece of a broiled fish, and of an honeycomb. And he took *it,* and did eat before them.

John 20: 24-29

But Thomas, one of the twelve, called Didymus, was not with them when Jesus came. The other disciples therefore said unto him, We have seen the Lord.

But he said unto them, Except I shall see in his hands the print of the nails, and put my finger into the print of the nails, and thrust my hand into his side, I will not believe.

And after eight days again his disciples were within, and Thomas with them: *then* came Jesus, the doors being shut, and stood in the midst, and said, Peace *be* unto you.

Then saith he to Thomas, Reach hither thy finger, and behold my hands; and reach hither thy hand, and thrust *it* into my side: and be not faithless, but believing.

And Thomas answered and said unto him, My Lord and my God.

Jesus saith unto him, Thomas, because thou hast seen me, thou hast believed: blessed *are* they that have not seen, and *yet* have believed.

After these things Jesus shewed himself again to the disciples at the sea of Tiberias; and on this wise shewed he *himself*. John 21: 1-6, 9, 12-14.

There were together Simon Peter, and Thomas called Didymus, and Nathanael of Cana in Galilee, and the *sons* of Zebedee, and two other of his disciples.

Simon Peter saith unto them, I go a fishing.

They say unto him, We also go with thee.

They went forth, and entered into a ship immediately; and that night they caught nothing. But when the morning was now come, Jesus stood on the shore: but the disciples knew not that it was Jesus.

Then Jesus saith unto them, Children, have ye any meat?

They answered him, No.

And he said unto them, Cast the net on the right side of the ship, and ye shall find.

They cast therefore, and now they were not able to draw it for the multitude of fishes.

As soon then as they were come to land, they saw a fire of coals there, and fish laid thereon, and bread.

Jesus saith unto them, Come *and* dine.

And none of the disciples durst ask him, Who art thou? knowing that it was the Lord.

Jesus then cometh, and taketh bread, and giveth them, and fish likewise. This is now the third time that Jesus shewed himself to his disciples, after that he was risen from the dead.

Then the eleven disciples went away into Galilee, into a mountain where Jesus had appointed them. And when they saw him, they worshipped him: but some doubted. Matthew 28: 16-18, 20.

And Jesus came and spake unto them, saying, All power is given unto me in heaven and on earth . . . I am with you alway, *even* unto the end of the world.

Mark 16: 15, 17, 18

And he said unto them, Go ye into all the world, and preach the gospel to every creature. And these signs shall follow them that believe; In my name shall they cast out devils; they shall speak with new tongues; they shall take up serpents; and if they drink any deadly thing, it shall not hurt them; they shall lay hands on the sick, and they shall recover.

I Cor. 15: 6, 7

After that, he was seen of above five hundred brethren at once; . . . After that he was seen of James; then of all the apostles.

Acts 1: 4

And being assembled together with *them,* commanded them that they should not depart from Jerusalem, but wait for the promise of the Father, which,

Luke 24: 49-51

saith he, ye have heard of me. And, behold, I send the promise of my Father upon you: but tarry ye in the city of Jerusalem, until ye be endued with power from on high.

And he led them out as far as to Bethany, and he lifted up his hands, and blessed them. And it came to pass, while he blessed them, he was parted from them, and carried up into heaven.

Hebrews 12: 1, 2

Wherefore seeing we also are compassed about with so great a cloud of witnesses, let us lay aside every weight, and the sin which doth so easily beset *us,* and let us run with patience the race that is set before us, looking unto Jesus the author and finisher of *our* faith; who for the joy that was set before him endured the cross, despising the shame, and is set down at the right hand of the throne of God.